T

Autumn is
Here!

Michael Herschell

Illustrated by

Shirley Tourret

4

Yes, it's an autumn mist.

It's often misty on autumn mornings. The mist goes away when the sun comes out.

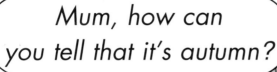

7

In autumn the leaves on the trees turn yellow, orange, brown and red.

9

In autumn the leaves fall off some trees.

The strong, autumn winds are
called gales.
The gales blow the leaves
off the trees.

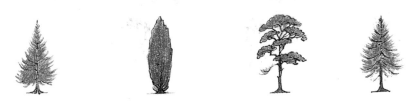

Some trees are called
evergreens because they
stay green all year round.
Evergreens often have
needles instead of leaves.

16

We often have bonfires in
the garden in autumn.

These berries are called
rosehips. They are the fruit
of the rose bush.

19

20

Apples and pears ripen
in autumn.

21

Look at all the birds sitting in a row.

Those are swallows. They are getting ready to fly away.

22

In autumn lots of birds
migrate to warmer places.

In autumn the farmer stores
food and bedding for
the animals in the barn.

In the winter the animals
will need food to eat and
bedding to sleep on.

In autumn squirrels
store nuts and acorns to eat
during the winter.

In autumn it gets dark
earlier in the evenings.

These are things we see in
autumn.
Can you name them?